Revolt of the Masscult

Revolt of the Masscult

Chris Lehmann

PRICKLY PARADIGM PRESS
CHICAGO

Prickly Paradigm Press, LLC
5629 South University Avenue
Chicago, Il 60637

www.prickly-paradigm.com

ISBN: 0-9717575-7-7
LCCN: 2002115994

Printed in the United States of America on acid-free
paper.

Mass culture: the very words conjure bygone eras of unthinkable self-seriousness. To confess a belief that there *is* such a thing as mass culture is akin to reporting sasquatch sightings or alien abductions. It is simply not done—to advance this, or for that matter any, faintly invidious category of cultural description. By common acclamation we are now in an age when the old hierarchies of taste are toppled, when the makers and promoters of all manner of media and entertainment have opened wide the gates that closed out marginalized forms of identity and experience from the realm of timeless thought and expression. Not for us the agonies of American writers and critics who beheld in the rise of mass culture the erosion of public debate, the debauching of an educated citizenry, the collapse of national memory and (not least by a longshot) the free fall in the quality of our own imaginative strivings, national epics and democratic aspirations.

But like most taboo subjects, mass culture will not stay put for its own post mortems—indeed, its absence from contemporary debate is a far more telling symptom of the need to repress it than a vindication of its alleged obsolescence. It is, after all, everywhere, regardless of how we choose to name it—since mass culture is, above all, the culture of market prerogative, blotting out nearly all elements of individual taste with prefigured consensus. In the music industry, mass marketing has all but erased honorable canons of taste, fusing most new product into a single all-purpose, soundalike genre—spun only for the sake of radio formatting into pop, country, and R & B markets. In the film industry, the mass mandate of product homogenation forces character and plot into a bleak template of mere exposure, paring down human nature to the urges to maim, seduce, humiliate and dominate. In the publishing world, mass promotion strategies script a relentless march of Tom Clancys, Danielle Steels and Wally Lambs through the national attention span. In television—still the signature medium for mass cultural expression—real living fellow citizens are now routinely conscripted into serial rites of exploitation and self-humiliation. And we the audience are left to assuage the uneasy suspicion that this resembles nothing so much as Roman bloodsport with the odd consolation that the participants have contracted to exchange their self-respect for money.

We can no longer call this depressing complex of forces "mass culture" even though they continue to bear all of mass culture's defining traits: rampant formal imitation, within and across genres; the recourse to formulaic stereotypes at the expense of inwardly developed character or subjectivity; instant stimulation at the expense of reflection or considered argument; and the lockstep choreography of one-dimensional emotional responses by turns sentimental and cynical.

Instead, in a little-discussed but greatly revealing semantic shift, the stuff of mass culture is now uniformly dubbed "popular," and the reflexive use of "popular culture" to denote the culture of the market leaves us all under the comforting impression that all mass entertainments are as freely chosen as, say, our political leaders or our forms of worship. This casual elision speaks volumes about the distance our culture has traveled since writers and critics heatedly debated the value of mass culture in the middle decades of the twentieth century. We have dispensed with generations of anxiety by an elegant incantation: Mass culture *is* culture; all culture is popular.

As a result of this numbing consensus, we can no longer coherently distinguish between a self-cre-ated cultural life and a merely manufactured one. The market, which has for so long decimated a vast range of social goods, from public education to public utili-ties, now also arbitrates the more intimate properties of our taste, culture and belief. We make our mass cul-ture behave like popular culture the moment we forfeit the prosaic understanding of its production, distribution and transmission. So it is of no real consequence, for instance, that broadcasting executives cribbed the American brand of reality television from a smattering of ghoulish and voyeuristic European shows. No, reality TV branded itself overnight into the heart of "our" popular culture, and so rather than discussing patterns of market predation or the human rights trespasses involved in mass voyeurism and total surveillance broadcasting, we all dutifully rallied to the question of what dark reaches of "our" national soul the new ghoulish turn in programming was baring.

Likewise, the weary spectacle of faux-transgressive arts controversies—themselves telling instances of the massification of former high culture—are treated as epic clashes of American taste communities, a heartbeat removed from *Inherit the Wind*. Insurgent artists, laying their brave hands on defensive pieties and oppressive orthodoxies, are held to smash the cherished icons and offend the dreary sensibilities of the Middle American believe-oisie. Never mind that the most recent such variation on this tired theme, the 1999 Brooklyn Arts Museum's "Sensations" exhibit, was a lavish spectacle of corporate arts underwriting, assembled under the aegis of an ad executive and wooed across the Atlantic by a second-tier venue pursuing the quite deliberate aim of raising its own profile with the publicity that a segmented-shark and Madonna-in-dung exhibit was certain to generate. The individual artists featured were also no strangers to corporate troughs: Damien Hirst, purveyor of the carved critter art, is far from an incendiary rebel; he is, rather, a trendy London restauranteur. And Chris

Offili, the artist who had created the porn-and-shit-spangled Madonna portrait at the center of the fuss, had earlier shown his daring artistic mettle with a dung-encrusted sculpture of an Absolut Vodka bottle—bearing the sponsor-osculating title "Imported"—in a London exhibition the distillery had commissioned as a virtual ad campaign. For a didactic tableau in "controversial" art, the BAM episode was as short on actual aesthetic transgression as it was on an interested viewing public.

Nor, alas, is this kind of confusion confined to cultural matters. In political life, too, the deft transmutation of clumsy mass manipulation into the image of popular choice is very much the stock in trade. This is especially the case in the polity of the present age, which routinely transmutes all matter of political conflict—from Bill Clinton's impeachment to the War on Terrorism—into broad, and invitingly inconclusive, questions of cultural self-definition. Most notoriously, of course, the ballot-challenged outcome of the 2000 presidential vote, instead of provoking serious discussion of a money-drenched, voter-repelling electoral process, bequeathed to legions of grateful pundits a simple diptych of an allegedly unfordable cultural chasm. There were, overnight, two Americas emerging before our eyes: the Gore-ist "Blue America" of the debauched relativist seaboards (and upper Midwest); and the Bushian "Red States" of the noble heartland interior, Sunbelt and South. Thus instructed in our new geography-is-destiny vision of cultural-cum-political conflict, we have gone on to diagnose symptoms of incorrigible cultural difference in everything from the popularity of NASCAR and professional wrestling (both surefire signs of "red state" habitation) to liberal media bias and "politically correct" canon-shredding (telltale signs of snobbish "blue state" reflexes). Even as cultural distinctions are emptied of meaning, they have become overloaded with alleged political import. It almost seems that the more trivial a question of cultural preference is, the more politicized it becomes.

ELITISM WITHOUT ELITES

Given this state of affairs, it's hardly surprising that any individual use of cultural distinction is taken to be an act of tremendous political faithlessness. For all the world-shaking import we now attribute to cultural life, no one seriously pursues critical distinctions *within* the study of culture—those outmoded judgments that rate, rank, and qualify the content, quality and intended audience for cultural production. Such distinctions have expired from common use because they are themselves widely taken to be blunt instruments of antidemocratic "elitism"—itself a curious, oversimplified term, since it is almost never linked to an identifiable formation of "elites." Philip Rahv used to complain that he didn't believe in the existence of a New Left because he never knew what its mailing address was; what, then, are we to make of the mysterious cabal of taste-stratification? The shadowy elites of today's cultural disputes apparently wield all sorts of unilateral cultural power, but they have neglected to adopt an organizational identity, an organ of opinion or a public spokesman.

They only seem to exist, indeed, in the heated rhetoric of culture combat. Try telling the editors of, say, *The New Criterion* that they're elitists for upholding bygone standards of judgment and excoriating postmodern and/or "outsider" experimentation in the arts, and you'll be told that, far from it, they are heroically defying the out-of-touch elites atop the universities, in the deconstruction-happy humanities departments and the anti-American curatorial establishment. Try out the same charge on, say, the Modern Language Association board or the editors of *Bad Subjects*, and you'll receive the same reply, only reverse coded, as in a photographic negative: They are subverting the dominant paradigms of taste, substituting the sympathetic view of agency-driven "audience reception" for insulting theories of passive culture consumption. And it's the traditionalist virtuecrats— right-wing crusaders against porn, free Web expression, and all things '60s—who are hell-bent on stifling the voice of the people.

To grasp how profoundly *un*challenging these oddly interlocking precepts of cultural posturing are in practice, merely consult the most recent redoubt in which something like an issue of cultural definition was actually joined: novelist Jonathan Franzen's public flaying for expressing misgivings about the cultural value of the nation's single greatest colossus of taste-marketing, the Oprah Winfrey Book Club. In September 2001, Franzen's novel *The Corrections* had been designated the Club's choice for the following month, and per the usual protocols of the show, a special segment had already been filmed, in which Franzen accompanied Oprah on a guided tour of his childhood haunts in St. Louis.

The only trouble was that Franzen, who was clearly quite new to the demands of round-the-clock book promotion, gave a handful of interviews in which wondered aloud whether the Oprah Book Club was an unalloyed force for the good. As a writer "solidly in the high art literary tradition," Franzen said (in an interview with the *Portland Oregonian*) that the Oprah selection "heightens this sense of split I feel.... I like to read entertaining books and this maybe helps to bridge that gap, but it also heightens these feelings of being misunderstood." In Franzen's other "controversial" interview on the Oprah pick—with the Powell's book-store web site—he first broached the question with a bit of indie-rock self-mockery. Asked about the Oprah pick, he replied: "Now that I've signed a big label deal and I'm playing stadiums, how good can I be?" He then went on to deride the notion of indie authenticity as only another marketing exercise in narrowcasting:

> One of the perverse, not to say fetishistic responses
> to the obliterative ubiquity of buying in our lives [is]
> to say, 'I don't buy the popular stuff, I buy the small

label stuff,' as if that makes you any less of a consumer. But I'm somewhat guilty of it myself and it
follows a pattern. Certainly in music, suddenly the
band you like because it was *not* produced goes to a
major label and becomes heavily produced.... But
I'm with you, I don't think the same applies to fiction. The problem in this case is some of Oprah's
picks. She's picked some really good books, but she's
picked enough schmaltzy, one-dimensional ones that
I cringe, myself, even though I think she's really
smart and she's fighting the good fight. And she's an
easy target.
But as far as being popular, yeah, I think Dave Barry
is really funny. And *Silence of the Lambs* is a really
smart book. But anyone who's sold out and been co-
opted, as I obviously have, says the same thing, and
it makes for a pathetic spectacle.

All this bears rehearsing at some length
because, in the tumult that followed upon these
remarks, scarcely anyone noted their substance.
Franzen may not have expressed himself with utmost
clarity. But what he's trying to do is not to elevate
himself above the mass-culture fray, as his many literary and journalistic assailants would have it. Rather,
he's doing what writers have been doing since they dis-
covered their vocation in an increasingly literate and
industrial social order some three and a half centuries
ago: He is making critical distinctions, few of which
he's impugning to his own advantage. His opening
ruminations on indie-rock authenticity, for example,
are there to remind his interviewer of how he *doesn't*
think of fiction as fodder for knee-jerk hipster derision
of sellouts and mainstream production values. And his

diction in his pronouncement on the schmaltzy ele-
ment of Oprah's taste shows him to be, if anything,
"populist" to a fault. ("*I cringe, myself*," i.e. as
someone who "likes to read entertaining books" and
who sees through the "fetishistic responses" that leave
all cultural audiences, regardless of their own earnest
self-regard, at a loss to be "any less of a consumer.")
Finally, his last, off-the-cuff litany of popular pleasures
are again offered in the spirit of self-parody, high-
lighting the futility of making such gestures of mollifi-
cation toward a mass-cultural market that's already
absorbed him. It's "a pathetic spectacle" to dramatize
your own writerly fondness for popular cultural productions, since it can be readily confirmed that such
protestations are the surefire mark of getting "sold out
and co-opted."

From what one might make out of the next
several months of media coverage, however, it was as
though Franzen had donned a high waistcoat and
periwig and loudly professed himself a loyal subject of
the Queen. Media commentators whose sense of good
sportsmanship corresponds roughly to that of English
soccer mobs took all their cues not from the lone culture creator and his carefully striated understanding of
how mass audiences and illusions of cultural authenticity feed off each other. No, they were on the side of
Oprah—which meant, in the curious alchemy by
which our culture wars unfold, that they were on the
side of The People.

And Oprah, for her part, made sure the lines of
conflict were drawn as quickly and sharply as possible.
In a fit of pique, Dame Winfrey officially dis-invited

Franzen from his scheduled studio appearance, though *The Corrections* remained a Book Club pick and a best-seller. Once Oprah supplied the lead, nearly every commentator on the affair duly pilloried Franzen as a hateful snob. Here was the phantom elitist who has haunted many a postwar cultural debate made flesh at last, uttering those perfidious, invidious words "schmaltzy" and "one dimensional." And most damning of all, there was Franzen's smoking-gun: "high art literary tradition"—that foppish preserve of Old World self-regard in which our ungrateful cox-comb of a novelist presumes to be "solidly" a member in good standing. (Franzen would later try to explain that this most damning of locutions was in fact his sleep-deprived effort to say "high modernist tradi-tion"—though it's not clear that this would have mat-tered much, since the term "high" is what set so many commentators a-fulminating, suggesting as it does the outrageous assertion that some cultural traditions are actually better than others.)

Franzen's transformation into an Enemy of the People was instantaneous. The *Oregonian* ran its initial Franzen interview under the wan headline, "Oprah's Stamp of Approval Rubs Writer in Conflicted Ways," little sensing its true world-shaking cultural import. In one typical high-populist oration two weeks later, a signed *New York Times* editorial dubbed Franzen "The Not-Ready-for-Prime-Time Novelist" condemning him in rapid order for his remarks, for living in "a solipsistic dream world" and for courting a readership composed of "people who buy books mainly to adver-tise their intellectual independence." (What else, after

all, could any reader professing ambivalence about
mass culture *be*?)

Franzen's fellow writers were, if anything,
harsher in their histrionics: Andre Dubus III railed
that Franzen's posture in the affair "is so elitist that it
offends me deeply," apparently eager to shoehorn as
many empty and fashionable protestations of cultural
grievance into a single sentence as he could. But he
was, in truth, only warming up: "The assumption that
high art is not for the masses, that they won't understand it and they don't deserve it—I find this repre-
hensible," Dubus sputtered to *New York Times* reporter
David Kirkpatrick, even though Franzen neither said
nor implied any such thing. "Is that a judgment on his
audience? Or on the books in whose company his
would be?" That oddly overgrammatical closing
flourish served to remind attentive readers that Dubus
himself was a prior Oprah pick, for his novel *House of
Sand and Fog*, and so might be presumed to be wan-
dering into a little solipsistic dream world of his own.

THIS WONDERFUL, VERTICALLY INTEGRATED WOMAN

The real fire and brimstone, however, rained down from the publishing industry proper, which lives and dies by blockbuster marketing strategies and so of necessity must regard Ms. Winfrey as nothing less than a secular saint. "When I ever even come close to voicing any sympathy [for Mr. Franzen], I am actually shouted down," one anonymous, shaken book editor confided to the *New York Observer*'s Gabriel Snyder, "even with people I am intimate with, who would tell me the truth." One book editor dismissed Franzen's views with the pithy aperçu "I'd like to punch the motherfucker," while another's foray into populist cultural theorizing produced this: "This wonderful woman devotes a portion of her daytime program to praise-songs to particular novels that not only bring news of literature to an area of broadcasting that was totally devoid of it, but that manages to motivate hundreds of thousands—even millions—of readers to go out and buy that book, and the literary world has a problem with this? I mean, in its darkest terms, that's insane."

Well, no, actually. For a real dose of insanity, ponder the (not-so) tacit reasoning by which this source—a cultural gatekeeper of considerably more influence in America's market-mad arbitration of taste than Franzen could ever presume to be—blithely assumes that mass audiences need a charismatic leader ("this wonderful woman") to deliver "news of literature" into their poor cavernous noggins, propped as they are slack-jawed for days on end before "an area of broadcasting that was totally devoid of it." Note as well that this Maximum Cultural Leader's "praise songs" motivate not just hundreds of thousands, but millions— *millions!*—of readers to go out and purchase the books she endorses. This, too, leaves a towering apprehension of stereotyped low-market taste selection magisterially intact. It's a presumption so blinding that its adherents likely don't even notice they're perpetuating it as they sing their Whitmanian hymns for the People on Oprah's behalf. (Or is it vice versa?) But it becomes plain enough if you pause a moment and imagine transplanting the argument into other settings. Just think, for instance, what furor would ensue if this righteous editor were to suggest that not merely mass audiences, but whole financial sectors trembled with uncritical adulation of Alan Greenspan, Warren Buffett, or Bill Gates due to orchestrated campaigns of cultural bullying—even though this is far closer to a statement of truth than the arch and condescending myth that Oprah, Mighty Oprah, by herself has bestowed blessed literacy upon the millions condemned to the outer darkness in the benighted American heartland.

It's a curious dynamic, to put things mildly, when a Jonathan Franzen gets excoriated for "elitism" in terms like this—conferring one-sided, culture-arbiting powers to a one-woman colossus. Recall, as well, that Franzen did not in any way disown Oprah's actual contributions to the literary market but rather was merely expressing an ambivalence about his own Oprah selection. He had taken care in all his statements to stipulate that she was healthfully promoting literature and an "easy target." One might expect people who prize literacy also to acknowledge that ambivalence is, or should be, the very sort of sentiment we should expect from a fiction writer. But that sentiment, like the taste distinctions Franzen forwarded about himself and his work, might as well have been uttered in Urdu.

These might seem like semantic quibbles, but the culture that can neither credit nor acknowledge the force of cultural distinctions—particularly in the world of literary discourse—is in sorry shape. Ironically enough, the direst implications for it reside in the question of its democratic make-up—the very ground that Franzen's lusty attackers are presuming to defend. For it is, in truth, a far more democratic impulse to insist on cultural distinctions, taste judgments and the autonomy of culture from market forces—and a far more troubling one to chart the nation's cultural well-being on the undeviating axis of how writers and readers alike can best display their gratitude to a single arbiter of taste.

This core paradox dilates into absurdity when one examines the anything-but-controversial elevation of another literary eminence, at the very moment when the Oprah-Franzen tempest was at its fullest fury. In October, Trinidanian novelist V.S. Naipaul was named the 2001 Nobelist for literature. Throughout his career, Naipaul has given great offense to all sorts of literary figures and audiences—to say nothing of entire religious traditions and ethnic groups. Not long before his elevation to The Nobel-itry, in a long interview with Farrukh Dondhy in the *Literary Review*, Naipaul denounced E. M. Forster as a sodomite and a liar; in a *Washington Post* profile shortly after being awarded the prize, he joked that Hindu Indian women sported bindis because "it means 'my head is empty,'" celebrated his youthful dalliances with prostitutes, and suggested that the kind of people who called in to the show of public radio literary personality Diane Rehm (on which he had just appeared) were not the kind who read his novels; indeed, he has no truck with any such "limited people" who lack "longer views in their minds" and have "no culture."

Needless to say, Naipaul earned no sober rebukes from *Times* editorialists or righteous lectures from fellow novelists or profane derision from publishing sachems—even though his remarks were much less qualified and much more openly insulting than Franzen's were. Indeed, the laureate's many outbursts were (and continue to be) simply written down to the "contrarian" prerogative of the celebrity author. And that is entirely proper: If a writer wants to issue provocative, even brazenly offensive, views, that's part of his job—and it's a healthy precept of any cultural democracy that the general reading public can handle ill-considered writerly opinions like grownups.

But set in relief beside the unruly populist pile-ons occasioned by Franzen's mild dissents, Naipaul's utterances help underline a central tenet of our new cultural dispensation. Tell your own listening audience that they're limited people and you're challenging their cultural presumptions. Disdain entire classes of women or believers and it's only an impish, perhaps even a brave, feint at the iron institutional bulwarks of "political correctness." But sin against the market— suggest you might try exercising some actual taste distinctions against the tidal onrush of literary promotion strategies—and you are a rank elitist. None of this is to suggest that Naipaul—truly a splendid novelist— should have come in for the sort of public garroting that Franzen got. But it is to remind us of the premier rule of engagement in contemporary cultural warfare: The market is always right.

THE MASSCULT MAKEOVER

How did we reach this pass? As the rise of mass culture in the 1920s began to preoccupy writers and critics, they devoted a great deal of effort to distinguishing the ephemeral stuff of market meritriciousness from the more demanding aesthetic productions that made for a genuine cultural tradition. Many of these categorical judgments were heatedly debated—as is often the case in matters of taste. But what's important to remember is that they were taken very seriously, precisely as a conundrum for a formal democracy evolving its own mass culture. The masscult question ripened into a full-fledged debate in postwar America: Most observers on either side viewed it through the lens of the Cold War, when America felt beset by raging totalitarian *Kulturkampfs*. Since the experience of World War II had so recently shown national cultures to be an instrument of the worst kind of political repression, it was painfully evident that culture came freighted with rather momentous political import. And conversely, it was just as clear—to masscult critics, anyway—that culture should help *determine* the character of democratic life, rather than serving as a passive vessel of its alleged expression.

Such was, indeed, the great preoccupation of leftist critic Dwight Macdonald, who emerged in the 1950s and '60s as one of the leading public foes of mass-culture consensus. He was also one of the most misunderstood then, and unappreciated now. Using the crude present-day calculus of cultural politics, many commentators now regard Macdonald as hopelessly fusty, conservative, and—yes—elitist. This case is almost never argued, but only inferred from the basic terms of Macdonald's analysis—his efforts, most of all, to clearly delimit the canons, aesthetic responses and social origins that mark the characteristic productions of *Masscult, Midcult and High Culture* (the title of his extended essay on the subject).

In reality, however, Macdonald's masscult criticisms issued largely from his own embattled position on the anti-Stalinist left, and sought to uphold the democratic value of independent taste-making. Macdonald wrote that culture was not imperiled so much by the alleged vulgarity of its consumers as by the magisterial presumptions exercised on their behalf by its gatekeepers. "A masochistic underestimation of the audience for good work in every field, even movies, even television, is typical of the American cultural entrepreneur," Macdonald wrote. "Some good movies have made money, after all, and many bad ones, though concocted according to the most reliable formulae, have failed to. Nobody really knows and it seems more democratic... to assume that one's own audience is on one's own level than that they are the 'hypothetical dolts' which both the businessmen of Hollywood and the revolutionaries of the Universities and *Left Review* assume they are."

Alien as such a notion may be to our own market-bewitched ears, the argument against mass culture was animated largely by just this faith in the integrity and the aspirations of the audience. In Macdonald's case, this translated into a refusal even to believe in the lowest-common-denominator construct of a "mass man," since this was an enabling fiction that *anti*democratic political movements found it most convenient to embrace: "To become wholly a mass man would mean to have no private life, no personal desires, hobbies, aspirations or aversions that are not shared by everybody else. One's behavior would become entirely predictable, like a piece of coal, and sociologists could at last make up their tables confidently.... Nazism and Soviet Communism... show us how far things can go [toward this end] in politics, as Masscult does in art."

Macdonald's masscult dissent was also (and continues to be) a position that insists that something vital is at stake in understanding cultural life as an autonomous realm of expression and debate. Self-styled populist defenders of masscult dismiss this notion as art-for-art's-sake "elitism," but this misses the key consideration. By recognizing culture as an autonomous realm of inquiry, with its own, ever-debatable standards and taste distinctions, we don't sunder the substance of cultural distinction from a democratic politics. Rather, we furnish ourselves with the means to judge the experiential payoffs of formal democracy as it takes on the characteristics of a mass society. Is mass culture, like mass politics, likely to make a more open and just social order easier to imagine? Do the objects of cultural consensus work to enable dissent and debate or nullify them? Would new forms of mass communication—television, most notably—dramatically reduce the range of ideas that come into play for public discussion, or expand them?

And perhaps most critically, would the drift away from "high" culture rupture the ordinary citizen's most basic sense of historical continuity? The whole point of speaking about culture, after all, is to invoke a legible tradition of inquiry, argument and letters, whose central features continue to change over time. As Macdonald justly put it, one of the gravest menaces facing inhabitants of the postwar world was an encroaching pastlessness. One of the signal offenses of midcult—the dumbed down renovations of high culture undertaken by Archibald Macleish, Mortimer Adler, Norman Rockwell, and other "lapsed avant-gardists"—Macdonald observed, was its violence to "the historical sense... that feeling for the special quality of each moment in historical time which, from Vico to Spengler, has allowed us to appreciate the past on its own terms." Citing both the Stalinist drive to eradicate all pre-Communist history and the giddy midcult compulsion to clumsily update the materials of the Western canon, Macdonald concluded glumly that "a people which loses contact with its past becomes culturally psychotic."

POP AND PASTLESSNESS

You don't have to look far to see how widely this psychosis has spread in the sunny masscult consensus of our own age. It is, indeed, the m.o. of consumer society to keep the buying self in a chronic state of forgetfulness, so that more and more of the same marketed blandishments can continue to appear new and life-transforming. At the same time, however, masscult has to be amnesia-friendly without being in any way upsetting. Hence the proliferation of comforting masscult productions that reference half-remembered—and camp-inflected—earlier epochs in mass culture, repurposed across genre lines. With an overabundance of things to see and consume, audiences now get brusquely niche-marketed toward an aesthetic of warmed-over familiarity, giving new substance to critic Clement Greenberg's complaint about the "predigested" formal qualities of kitsch.

The senescent popular art form of the Broadway musical, for example, now typically tries to market itself to mass audiences by pillaging the archives of Hollywood for repurposed content. Indeed, the production that has revived the genre, "The Producers," began life as a movie that caustically sent-up the debased standards of... Broadway musical productions. "The Sweet Smell of Success," a mordant study in the moral decline of all things journalistic and entertainment-minded, and one of the most cynical American movies ever produced, has undergone a similar odyssey (albeit with far less pleasing critical and commercial results), as have still lesser movie-cum-musicals, such as "Thoroughly Modern Mille," "Hairspray," and "The Full Monty."

Meanwhile, in Hollywood proper, studios appear to be sunk irretrievably into amnesiac nostalgia and formulaic sequel, prequel, and empty televisual crossover. A recent *New York Times* report on the summer 2002 movie season disclosed no less than 16 repurposed plot vehicles, cribbed from an omnivorous range of templates. These include cannibalized comic strip characters (*Spiderman*), live-action versions of animated children's TV shows (*Scooby-Doo*); and cable adventure fare made film (*The Crocodile Hunter: Collision Course*). In another woozy study in reverse-synergy, one such predigested entry—*The Scorpion King*, rather desperately ginned up from a minor villain featured in an earlier sequel, *The Mummy Returns*—is furnishing the pretext for a cable TV documentary: "Although the film is entirely fictional," we are assured in the comforting cadence of Timespeak, "it is loosely based on the legend of an actual ancient figure. This is allowing the History Channel to piggyback on the film's release by showing a new documentary... about 'The Real Scorpion King.' And not only that, but research by Egyptologists about the legendary king will be part of the documentary."

"Not only that" is a perfect touch—registering the genteel befuddlement of our *Times* correspondent that, in the midst of this riot of cross-branding, a documentary could still feature *actual historical authorities*! "Psychosis" may be too dignified a term for the unimaginative production of so much inert and unchallenging mass entertainment. This aesthetic of derivative pseudofamiliarity is, of course, anything *but* the apprehension of history. If anything, these faux-nostalgic rehabilitions of past masscult eras domesticate the idea of the past into nothing more than a harmless plaything for terminally unaffiliated mass audiences. In the bright pastel glow of the Austin Powers franchise, the '60s, far from an era of riots, civil rights marches, and antiwar strife, become a time of empty, horny modishness. The seventies are no longer the decade of scandal, stagflation, fuel shortages, and national malaise, but the time of *Scooby-Doo* and the oversatiated deadpan sensibilities that propel *Boogie Nights, That '70s Show*—and, of course, that most self-cannibalizing of all TV productions, *The Rerun Show*.

This, too, may seem like harmless fluff—isn't nostalgia always as much an exercise in forgetting as remembering? And shouldn't it be that much more the case when past masscult eras are being ridiculed for their quaint cluelessness? But emptying even the recent past of recognizable political content leaves culture consumers with the sense that American society has always been the same placid sensorium that it looks to be from the comforts of the den or the Multiplex. And this, in turn, mirrors the homogeneity of much of one's own subjective, lived experience. With no clear sense how one's own understandings of how one's family, life trajectories, and tastes have changed over time, the American self remains an infinitely suggestible work-in-progress, prey to both commodified reveries of self-reinvention and endless waves of revived kitsch.

THE MARKET, YES

Yet for all their perspicacity, Macdonald and other partisans of the masscult critique were wrong on a key point: the culprit responsible for our pitiable state of cultural amnesia was neither one of the hulking ideological formations of the Cold War, massed under the banners of communism and capitalism. It has been, rather, a creeping cultural populism. This has taken root, curiously enough, in a paint-by-numbers functionalist view of culture that's far more vulgar than the crudest of Marxist theories of cultural domination that the advocates of such populism cast themselves in heroic opposition to. Put simply, in the forty-some years since the masscult debate's heyday, mass culture has come to be deemed not merely a healthy adjunct force in American democracy, but the functional substitute for American democracy. As one communications revolution eclipsed another, the most meaningful choices afforded to Americans were deemed cultural ones—even though the actual production and distribution of these choices occur at the behest of an ever narrowing cartel of multileveraged, and multinational, corporate players. As one new political consensus rudely overturned another—as the Reagan Revolution succumbed to Third Way neoliberalism, which in turn fragmented blurrily into smaller wavelets of Gingrichism, "compassionate conservatism," and whatnot—the most telling differences and conflicts in American life were seen to flow out of cultural allegiances, devilishly protean in form and supposedly impassable in content.

The ground for the masscult makeover was cleared in no small way by the early dissent from mass-culture nay-saying that sociologist Edward Shils published in *The Sewanee Review* in 1957, "Daydreams and Nightmares." Shils straightforwardly reversed the poles that had determined the course of the debate thus far; he argued that mass culture, far from the fulfilling the bleak prophetic visions propounded by the Macdonalds, Clement Greenbergs and Richard Hoggarts of the world, was actually elevating the reading, viewing, and reasoning habits of the American culture consumer. This being the case, the criticism of mass culture was profoundly undemocratic, and in Shils' view, something far worse: It wasn't American. "The new critique of mass culture takes over many of the aristocratic and aesthetic arguments about the anti-bourgeois attitudes of

19th-century Europe," he wrote at the outset of his essay. Then, scarcely missing a beat, he ramped this rhetorical caricature up from aristocracy-coddling to full-on decadent Marxism. This was most especially the case with the intellectual cohort that, amazingly enough, still serves as the *bête noire* for cultural populists of all ideological persuasions 45 years after Shils' essay: the group of émigré scholars clustered around the Frankfurt School of Behavioral Sciences (or, as Shils insisted on dubbing it, with the clear aim of impressing upon readers its intransigent foreign-ness, "the *Institut*"). Shils argued that this woeful congeries of for-eigners—Max Horkheimer, Herbert Marcuse, Theodor Adorno and Erich Fromm—only took to inveighing against mass culture when the Nazis had driven them to the United States. "Here they encountered the 'mass' in modern society for the first time," Shils wrote in what he imagined to be acerbic bluster—even though, in both their scholarship and the condition of exile, they bore eloquent witness to their familiarity with the con-fluence of the "mass" in a society with the ugliest kinds of political repression.

Yet the actual continental genesis of "the *Institut*'s" masscult discontent need not detain a cultural patriot like Shils. Indeed, being German only makes these critics *more anti-American*: "Their anti-capitalistic, and by multiplication, anti-American attitude found a traumatic and seemingly ineluctable confirmation in the popular culture of the United States.... What is a vague disdain in Europe must become an elaborate loathing in America." The fretful Frankfurt fops, moreover, bring to the criticism of mass culture a grudge against the ordinary working *volk*, borne of their dalliances with radical politics. Once besotted with the role that Marx, Engels & Co. had roughed out for the common worker in the transformation of history, the critics of masscult are now afflicted with "the obsessiveness of the disappointed lover who, having misconceived his beloved when their love was blooming, now feels that she deceived him and he now has no eye for anything but her vices and blemishes."

Note Shils' creeping tone of historical determinism, which would go on to be a signature theme of cultural populist posturing: Much as their foreign birth foreordains that their whimpering over mass society's excesses in their homelands *must* become anti-American "loathing," so too does their posture of revolutionary disappointment determine that they act and write from "only the frustrated attachment to an impossible idea of human perfection, and a distaste for one's own society and for human beings as they are."

To insist that mass culture does not necessarily elevate its audiences, in other words, is to hate humanity. It is, moreover, a pathology of the antidemocratic mind, since, Shils argued, "the root of the trouble lies not in mass culture but in the intellectuals themselves.... It is not popular literacy and leisure which forces university professors to spend their leisure time in reading crime novels or looking at silly televisions programs. If they lower their standards, they should not blame those who have not had the privilege of living within a tradition of high standards such as they themselves enjoy or could enjoy if they cared to do so."

Shils also flogs a number of (now) long-familiar hobby-horses that are still trotted out and pummeled by latter-day masscultists eager to discredit the democratic bona fides of intellectual critics. He argues, for example, that there never had been a golden age of "high culture." Indeed, to profess a preference for past cultural apogees bespeaks a reflexive scorn that can, yes, "only" issue from "ignorance and prejudice, impelled by a passionate and permanent revulsion against [the masscult critics'] own age and own society."

Shils even undertakes an embryonic form of what is today widely celebrated as audience reception theory—the beguiling fancy that just because an idea or art object is subject to mass transmission doesn't mean that it's not subject to canny individualist appropriations of its political messages on the part of previously marginalized constituencies. Shils protests that under the present woeful dispensation of sociologists bewitched by the masscult critique, "the nature of the person who reads or hears some work of popular culture is inferred from the content of the work, on the assumption that every image, every event corresponds to some deep and central need in the personality of the reader, viewer or listener. There is no reason whatever to think that this is so." Indeed, in a flourish worthy of the flashy reversals of binary oppositions that have furnished no end of titles for no end of cultural studies monographs, Shils offered up this summary reading of this particular *trahison des clercs*: "The sociological study of mass culture is the victim of the culture of sociological intellectuals."

It was in vain, apparently, that critics like Macdonald and Greenberg argued for avant-garde and "high" culture as critical repositories of democratic experience that could rescue actual cultural debate from the bogs of uncritical masscult consensus. By presuming to tender any judgments about the content of mass culture, it turns out that, by Shils' lights and those of the many intellectual critics who followed in his wake, they were betraying the democratic triumph of its *form*. And still more insidiously, of course, they're raging hypocrites; the mere fact of "lowering their standards by reading crime novels or looking at silly television programs" shows them up as guilt-ridden snobs—even though it's an odd model of criticism that expects practitioners to proceed from a position of total ignorance of the genre.

It's instructive to weigh Shils' romantic depiction of the thwarted revolutionary passions of the mass culture critics against their actual profiles and commitments. Most of these people, after all, were bitter and convicted ideological foes of all Stalinist tendencies on the American left. This includes not merely the political journalists like Macdonald and Robert Warshow, but also their fellow dissenters on the more literary and philosphical left, such as Irving Howe, Mary McCarthy, Hannah Arendt, and Delmore Schwartz. All of them sacrificed a great deal more, both professionally and personally, for the sake of defying Stalinist orthodoxies than solemn professional diagnosers of their clinical malaise such as Shils ever had, or could.

But empirical considerations like these could never wreak serious harm on the Masscult

Counterrevolution. For all its readily detectable rhetorical distortions, Shils' argument was most noteworthy for its key formal breakthrough: He had assigned a tellingly elite and anti-American cast to the entire mass culture question, even as he sundered it from any intelligible economic moorings. This would go on to become one of the most fruitful procedures for insulating the rightward consensus in American politics and culture from any criticism, since in this closed system of thought, the act of criticism itself becomes unpardonably elitist, de facto evidence that your interlocutor thinks he's better than you. For Shils, mass culture was self-evidently democratic, and so all its critics were self-evidently authoritarian. The work of art, moreover, was little more than a vessel of preordained democratic virtue—as the product of American civilization. It simply *has* to be uplifting, by the same logic that dissenters in American civilization *have* to be perverse socialist-aristocrats. Or whatever they call them in the Old World.

This, too, was to become a signal paradox of latter-day culture warfare: by claiming the wrong kind of critics had politicized cultural questions, the defenders of Western tradition actually politicized it in ways far more potent—and far cruder—than any of their defeated adversaries could ever have intended. Culture gets subtly downgraded in the hands of putatively democratic defenders like Shils into an inert bearer of sunny partisan broadsides, monotonously reminding us that we live in the best of all possible worlds with the widest ambit of cultural choices, immune to most judgment and criticism. Culture, in the hands of masscult champions, becomes the political equivalent of mind cure—a functionalist array of pre-approved rhetorical gestures that, curiously enough, are never advocated by the elitist partisans on the other side of the masscult question.

From this sort of doublethink it's but a short step to the wholesale identification of culture *with* democracy. With the successive waves of pop art criticism and cultural studies scholarship that were to come in Shils' wake, most of the self-congratulatory populist reflexes on display in "Daydreams and Nightmares" became institutionalized orthodoxy. Across the fast-receding older lines of ideological conflict, commentators now agreed that terrible damage to democratic order would be wreaked when citizens exercised individual judgments of taste. By this logic, the masscult critics were depicted as short-circuiting the spontaneous satisfaction of wants and taste preferences that is the mark of a healthy democracy.

In an astonishingly prosaic tract called *Popular Culture and High Culture*, Herbert Gans—an academic of leftist leanings who one might assume was tailor-made to fit Shils' anti-intellectual caricature—actually went his fellow sociologist one better. Even Shils had to allow that mass culture was not the most edifying fare, and often an outright disappointment. But Gans would have none of it; indeed, he identified the true threat to democratic life not with the mass producers of kitsch but with the intellectual arbiters of high culture. And unlike Shils, he didn't diagnose this condition as a function of their perverse and alien radicalism, but rather as a sign of their decline in social prestige. Gans theorized that the appeal of the masscult critique corresponded with "the position of intellectuals in society, particularly those intellectuals who are and feel themselves part of the 'Establishment'; over time, the critique has appeared when intellectuals have lost power, and it has virtually disappeared when intellectuals have gained power and status." In the 1940s and '50s, the twin scourges of McCarthyism and suburban apathy provoked intellectuals into jeremiads against the masscult order. Gans glumly foresaw a renewed bout of masscult baiting in academic circles as the intellectual elite once again felt its status threatened by the leveling of the academic job market at a time when universities were also taking on new minority and women enrollments, and thereby—so Gans speculated—stirring new "fears" among high culture advocates that would spark new critiques of "egalitarian demands and of the Middle Americans who made them.... It is possible that the mass culture critique will be revived for use against the egalitarian trend."

And who would find egalitarian trends threatening, if not a gaggle of authoritarian intellectuals? Again and again, Gans makes passing reference to the never-specified project of "eliminating popular culture," at one point reminding readers that "it is impossible either to eliminate these [mass] media now or even to conceive a large modern society operating without them"—as though Dwight Macdonald was commanding a vast black-arm-banded legion of censors and TV-smashers. Indeed, in one typical flourish, he sanctimoniously manages to insinuate this motivation and charge the overwhelmingly socialist cohort of masscult critics with indifference to economic inequality and imperialist bloodletting: "Some critics who wish to banish the media and popular culture for their harmfulness seem much less interested in banning other phenomena which are actually much more harmful, including war and poverty." Of course, the only critic who came anywhere near the dread prospect of even hypothetically advocating the censoring (let alone the "banishing") of the nation's mass culture was the Frankfurt school philosopher Herbert Marcuse, who, to put things mildly, was much exercised over questions of war and poverty, being as he was a Marxist of the most strenuously committed variety. But apparently it's enough to impute *any* antidemocratic senti-ment—cultural, economic, militaristic, whatever—to this unnamed circle of masscult critics, since in the very act of criticism they have betrayed their true authori-tarian colors.

This dishonest procedure, like Shils' earlier bootless speculations on the fallacy of positing any bygone cultural golden ages and the virtues of audience reception theory, went on to attach itself with barnacle-like force to any and all ensuing discussions of mass culture. Well before Oprah set eyes on *The Corrections*, a long train of masscult critics, from Macdonald and Greenberg on the left to Peter Viereck and Allen Bloom on the right, were depicted as dangerous practi-tioners of the narrowest sort of cultural repression. But if masscult's pursuers were a composite portrait of Generals Franco and Kim Il Sung, longing to censor, starve and bomb their opponents into submission, so were its consumers granted every happy, democratic impulse of self-actualization, to the point of virtual parody. Gans theorized, for example, that "a housewife who has decided that she wants to decorate her home her own way, rather than in the way her parents and neighbors have always done" regards homemaking magazines as "not only a legitimation of her striving toward individual self-expression but an array of solutions from various taste cultures from which she can begin to develop her own."

Never mind, of course, that such magazines are outlets for legions of advertisers urging upon our striving homemaker a decorating regime involving commitments of upkeep, labor, and income far more suffocating than anything her meddling kin and neighbors could ever invent. And never mind that the average reader of such a magazine would never hew to a self-image so pitiful as to greet each new issue of *Good Housekeeping* as a premier outlet of "individual self-expression." Consider instead the world of presumption contained in Gans' insistence that this vital contact with a world of "new taste cultures" (i.e., mass-merchandised brands) permits the poor Hausfrau at last to "begin to develop her own."

This strategic placement of the hypothetical consumer at a tabula rasa point of taste acquisition can be superimposed perfectly upon our own age's theology of Oprah-mastered literacy: there, recall, no one in all of Middle America was thought to have used a book for any reason other than prying open the outhouse window before Oprah came along; here, the cringing American housewife is to be tutored in the barest rudiments of décor self-expression from the taste combines of *Better Homes and Gardens* and *Redbook*—underwritten by Johnson and Johnson and Colgate-Palmolive. She has to start somewhere, the poor dear.

Placing himself in the heroic posture of redeeming the market choices of ordinary Americans, Gans, like the scores of similarly situated academic theorists, cannot help revealing his own inadvertent condescension toward the masses he's empowering. And Gans is apparently not enough of a sociologist to consider that the oppressive yoke of Old World decorating tips that our model consumer is in the process of throwing off actually represents the outcome of a "taste culture"—more honestly come by, and in most cases much more prone to individual modification, than the spreads of interior-design porn awaiting her every month in the supermarket aisle.

As for the social revolution Gans saw brewing against masscult, spearheaded by vigilante posses of downwardly mobile academics, of course no such thing actually occurred. In fact, Gans' diagnosis of the immediate background of the postwar masscult uproar was woefully off-base, since the most virulent critics of masscult over the first flush of the Cold War were not aggrieved shabby genteel members of the Establishment, but lone journalist cranks such as Dwight Macdonald and defiantly independent academics such as Irving Howe. Intellectuals of the more Establishment persuasion, such as Daniel Bell and David Riesman, cheerfully greeted the triumph of masscult without serious complaint. In *The Lonely Crowd*, for example, Riesman did not, as is frequently supposed, deride the soullessness of mass conformism. Rather, he portrayed the malady of "other direction" as a transi-

tional condition that would open onto a new model of
Western character, organized around mass consumption
and free of outmoded "inner-directed" anxieties.
Riesman and his *Lonely Crowd* co-author Nathan Glazer
went so far as to propose the institution of shopping
curricula for the early elementary school student as a
means of smoothing the transition into full citizenship
of The Affluent Society.

What's more, the demographic upheavals in the
institutional life of the American mind that Gans saw as
a possible portent of a masscult backlash in fact produced the polar opposite effect: a runaway masscult
ecstaticism in the circles of higher learning. Beginning
in the 1980s, as tenured American culture critics began
experimenting with the Birmingham School's fledgling
theories of subcultural revolt as class politics by other
means, a stunning valorization of all American mass cultural expression was under way. The modern cultural
studies movement was born. Its disciplinary tributaries
varied—from semiotics to anthropology to comp lit on
through to mainstream humanities fields such as
English lit and history. But its reproduction across the
nation's campuses was strikingly homogenous.

It was, indeed, a subordinate irony of the '80s
cultural studies boom that, for all of its populist posturing it was gestating a genuine academic elite. The
explosion of cultural studies was as much institutional in
its conception as it was scholarly, forging a decades-long
boondoggle of professional credentialism, midwifing
new undergraduate divisions and multidisciplinary
administrative concentrations, even as its leading exponents tirelessly advertised their own curiously insular

radicalism and insatiable will-to-subversion. In the process, the always scarce resources of humanities divisions in American universities got distributed implacably upward, making the star system as much a signature of the world of higher learning as it is in the fields of sports, entertainment, and media. And much as in other professions, the consolidation of this elite coincided with a steady assault on lower-ranking members of the academic workforce, with teaching assistants and adjuncts undertaking the donkey work and heaviest teaching loads for next-to-nothing wages.

Even more strangely, this professionalization of masscult ecstasy ensured that its champions never encountered actual mass readerships. As culture critic Thomas Frank has observed, many of the early Cold War-era denunciations of mass culture, by contrast, went on to claim considerable popular audiences. In part of course, this was because they were overwhelmingly recruited from outside the academy, without its trademark lumbering prose and anxieties of influence. But one may well also assume that this interest credits the audiences and readerships in the cultural marketplace for exercising the sort of self-aware critical distinctions that people like Macdonald and Franzen have insisted upon all along. In other words, readers actually seem to prefer principled criticism over self-dramatizing populist celebrations of the market's might and wonder.

CULTURE FOR WHAT?

There's also a much deeper confusion at the heart of today's new masscult dispensation. In the crass instrumentalism of the Gans critique—the pragmatist presumption that whatever works is, by definition, culture, and hence due the deference of all good patriots—the logic of actual cultural life becomes inverted. Culture is that open-ended realm in which private tastes, disputations, entertainments, ideas, character, and beliefs all get tempered, argued through, and revised by contact with the wider public world. By designating an extra-official realm that allows us to tend to the making of aesthetic and moral sense, we can chart the shifting private satisfactions and public values we assign to the acts of writing, reading, composing—as well as the more ambiguously public enterprises of religious belief, philosophical reasoning, and social criticism. The broad ambit of culture enables us both to undertake the interpretation of these various kinds of expression and to understand ourselves functioning as its proper audience.

Making distinctions is obviously essential to all this cultural activity—and again, to the very idea of culture itself. As the critic Raymond Williams has argued, the notion of culture is defined by its claims to autonomy against the impersonal, coercive idea of society. That is to say, to speak of culture at all is to make a distinction—to invoke (comparatively) uncoerced creative enterprises over and above the more forceful, less affective and most decidedly *un*critical dispensations of the state, the corporation, and the market.

And this point opens, in turn, onto another key distinction now long submerged in the phony populism of American cultural debate: the critical roles of work and leisure in the already conflict-ridden business of making cultural sense. Many critics of '50s-era mass culture weren't principally exercised by its lurid content, or its philistine defenders; rather, they were troubled by the way that the wholly predictable unspooling of TV serials or formulaic mysteries mimicked the routines that culture consumers endured at the workplace. In both production and reception, culture is always a reflection of a healthy margin of leisure (as Russell Jacoby has pointed out, the word "school" comes from the Greek word for "leisure"); it supposes not merely an autonomous world of critical reasoning, but also the time and self-determination one needs to familiarize oneself with that world

Indeed, what remains compelling about the masscult critique, even at this late date, is the characterization of the undemanding culture of mass consumption as the flipside of the debased rounds of the American workday. Mass work and mass leisure were, by this view of things, a closed circle. It was not possible to understand the operation of the one without the other. Not only was the reception of a masscult psyche compensation for the no-less empty hours that consumers spent at their workplaces—the "faked sensations" that Clement Greenberg denounced in kitsch. Mass culture supplied working Americans also with one of the primary stables of images and ideas about the workplace and their life chances. Reviewing the results of a comparative survey of *Saturday Evening Post* biographical profiles between the years 1901 and 1941, Macdonald noted an inexorable march of celebratory fluff. Idle stargazing graced the magazine's pages at a 50 percent greater ratio in 1941, and the kind of celebrities profiled in the later year were purveyors of little more talent than their ability to smile. Whereas painters, opera singers, and the like rated serious attention at the turn of the century, in 1941 the magazine's personality studies were "*all* movie stars, baseball players and such; and even the 'serious' heroes in 1941 aren't so serious after all: the businessmen and politicians are freaks, oddities, not the really powerful leaders."

Macdonald argued that this monotonous array of merit-free public figurines completely contravened the self-made ideal type of American social mythology:

> [T]he modern *Satevpost* biographee is successful not because of his own personal abilities so much as because he 'got the breaks.' The whole competitive struggle is presented as a lottery in which a few winners, no more talented or energetic than anyone else, drew the lucky tickets. The effect on the mass reader is at once consoling (it might have been me) and deadening to effort and ambition (there are no rules, so why struggle?). It is striking how closely this evolution parallels the country's economic development... [as] the problem became how to consume goods rather than produce them.

As today's mass culture continues to serve as an elaborate random search generator of instant, disposable celebrity, these detached, fatalistic apprehensions of how achievement and reward operate in our society have been normalized apace. In the age of Enron, Worldcom and Global Crossing (to say nothing of Martha Stewart or *Survivor*), success is less than ever a function of working hard and getting ahead, and more than ever about cashing in and not getting caught.

The arrival of mass culture boded no less ill for the audience's already pinched uses of its own leisure. As its earliest critics argued, mass culture effectively wipes out the idea that either time or competence have anything to do with the transmission of culture. By imposing minimal demands on its audience, and downgrading the work of art into commodified sensation, masscult forced American leisure pursuits tightly into line with American workplace discipline. In his influential 1939 essay, "Avant-garde and Kitsch," *Partisan Review* art critic Clement Greenberg advanced one of the earliest versions of this critique. Kitsch, which called forth in debased mass formulas much the same aesthetic responses formerly demanded by high culture, was designed to satisfy the newly urbanized mass consumers who "learned to read and write for the sake of efficiency but... did not win the leisure and the comfort necessary for the enjoyment of the city's traditional culture," Greenberg wrote. "Discovering a new capacity for boredom... the new urban masses set up a pressure on society to provide them with a kind of culture fit for their own consumption." Thereupon followed Greenberg's famous rapid-fire litany of definitions of the monstrosity that was Kitsch:

> Kitsch, using for raw materials the debased and academicized simulacra of genuine culture, welcomes and cultivates this insensibility. It is the source of its profits. Kitsch is mechanical and operates by formulas. Kitsch is vicarious experience and faked sensations. Kitsch changes according to style, but always remains the same. Kitsch is the epitome of all that is spurious in the life of our times. Kitsch pretends to demand nothing of its customers except their money—not even their time. The precondition for kitsch, a condition without which kitsch would be impossible, is the availability close at hand of a fully matured cultural tradition, whose discoveries, acquisitions, and perfected self consciousness kitsch can take advantage of for its own ends. It borrows from it devices, tricks, stratagems, rules of thumb, themes, converts them into a system, and discards the rest. It draws its life blood, so to speak, from this

> reservoir of accumulated experience.... [It] predigests
> art for the spectator and spares him effort, provides
> him with a shortcut to the pleasures of art that
> detour what is necessarily difficult in the genuine
> art.

To present-day ears, attuned to the steady drone of populist *Kulturkampf*, this all sounds like a peroration on the unspeakable vulgarity of the Mass Man, an affront to all of American culture's democratic aspirations. But Greenberg, like MacDonald, rejected out of hand the construct of Mass Man as dangerously totalitarian; rather, as he wrote, he was seeking to define "the aesthetic experience as met by the specific—not general—individual." It was, indeed, the role of the avant-garde—the rarely discussed second term of Greenberg's landmark essay—to honor and sustain the discrete character of individual aesthetic experience, but he saw that the abstract formalism of the modernist avant-garde was working to sunder it fatally from its traditional audiences, and perhaps most fatally from its patron base, "an elite among the ruling class of that society from which [the avant-garde] assumed itself to be cut off, but to which it always remained attached by an umbilical cord of gold." This crisis of audience was triggering a genuine identity crisis for avant-garde culture: Even though "Picasso's shows still draw crowds and T.S. Eliot is taught in the universities.... the avant garde... is becoming more and more timid every day that passes." Like kitsch, avant-garde work was succumbing to mere formal mimicry of its own taste canons.

Ultimately, in Greenberg's view, the advance of kitsch and the retreat of the avant-garde culminated in a political crisis. With culture speaking to less and less of the urban masses' condition, Greenberg argued that they would train their social resentments against culture itself, via "a reactionary dissatisfaction which expresses itself in revivalism and puritanism, and latest of all, fascism." Hence he concludes his speculations with a dark, Goebbels-paraphrasing *envoi* entirely suited to the mood of the left culture critic in 1939: "Here revolvers and torches are mentioned in the same breath as culture. In the name of godliness or the blood's health, in the name of simple ways and solid virtues, the statue-smashing commences."

YES, WE HAVE NO IDEOLOGY

In retrospect, of course, this all seems a bit much—even though that suspicious klatsch of émigré intellectuals from Nazi Germany was already beginning to bear unnerving witness to the instrumentality of mass culture in fascism's rise. Still, as noted above, Greenberg, Macdonald and the kindred masscult critics loosely joined around "the *Institut*" erred in inscribing this—or, indeed, any—fixed ideological tendency to the transmission and reception of masscult. The industrial-pleasure complex is too slippery, too formally protean and too prone to demographic fragmentation to be outfitted handily with any crude agenda denoted with a single slogan—be it "the statue-smashing commences" or (its rhetorical flipside) "information wants to be free."

Which is not to say that masscult can be magically baptized a virtue, or a benign reflection of sovereign consumer choice, as has been the happy fate of so many other features of the post-Cold War American market frenzy. It does mean, however, that we need to rethink the played-out quality of so many of the terms that we've inherited to describe the masscult quandary.

Mass culture had never been all that effective a medium of direct agitprop for a particular political tendency. It has been, however, a compliant host organism for all the trademark themes of market consensus: the misanthropic contempt and undemanding sentimentality that informs most television plot trajectories; the cinematic vision of the self as a Hobbesian tangle of violent impulses; the general distrust of any emotional needs that won't be palliated by more shopping. The open celebration of these qualities is sufficiently depressing unto itself; but the fact that we are scarcely able to call them by their true names bears eloquent testimony to the decline and fall of anything resembling democratic cultural debate.

Historically, critics have depicted masscult's triumph as a process of Zombie-like stupefaction—which, in turn, has permitted the whole post-Gans cohort of masscult champions to score easy points by deriding the psychological crudities of the masscult critique. And at the same time, of course, the defenders of mass culture could pose as heroic champions of uncoerced audience reception. Many a contemporary intellectual makes a respectable living by hailing, à la Gans, the feeble gestures of masscult appropriation and subversion—gay-themed "Star Trek" chapbooks, luridly confessional daytime talk-shows, or the decades-long celebration of Madonna's many formulaic modes of consumer rebellion—as the vindication of marginal gender identities and obliquely allegorized political dissent.

Some of these misunderstandings might be cleared up if one lays aside the obsolete model of Borg-like masscult domination (whose chief exponents, such as Theodor Adorno and Frederic Wertham, are in any event many decades dead) and focuses instead on the heartbreakingly narrow range of these imagined shows of consumer autonomy. It does not oversimplify the logic by which masscult productions permeate our political thought—nor does it detract from the pleasures of zinedom, and other quaint byways of masscult dissent—to note the blinding paradox of supremely trivial gestures of resistance with disproportionately hulking ideological import. Indeed, one of the attractions of politicizing television programming with, say, faux-transgressive gender themes resides precisely in the cost-free nature of such interpretive transactions. Something as banal and formulaic as a TV show guarantees both that such gestures will be at once easy to perform and safely insulated from real-world political consequence. Moreover, politicizing these gestures in so broad a fashion robs them of their own clear virtue: their individuality, the bid to make one's own quirky and subjective sense of a TV serial or a pop star—i.e., the disposable stuff of kitschily commercial mass culture. Seeking to rescue "agency" in the drearily pre-

dictable rounds of consuming, cultural studies theo-
reticians ironically wind up draining it of any meaningful content—in a way that Greenberg and
Macdonald and company would have mordantly appre-
ciated.

FAILING SUBJECTS AND AVANT-ENCLOSURES

Subjectivity, indeed, is the realm in which masscult does its most insidious and least-noted damage. It's worth recalling, in this regard, that *1984*, our lead textual (if fictional) source for the depiction of the baleful rounds of modern propaganda-making, doesn't regard mass culture as the handmaiden of ideology—Oceana, after all, has effectively arrogated for itself the right to transmute the mandates of state into bald propaganda. Rather, in Orwell's dystopian vision, mass entertainment has mutated into something far creepier than ideological boilerplate: an orgy of nod-

wink-and-bray voyeurism, in which footage of terrible
disasters are transmitted on television for apprecia-
tively smug, hilarity-ridden mass viewerships in pubs,
cafes and private households. Now, of course, as all of
the features of Orwell's dystopia are dismissed by
readers who mistakenly took the book as a document
of social prophecy, this then-parodic vision has become
a dominant strain of our own age's masscult entertainment. Reality television most notoriously stimulates
and satisfies these unlovely appetites, be it the self-
abasing rituals of *Survivor* and *Big Brother*, the celebri-
tist *Schadenfreude* of *Fear Factor*, or intimacy-defiling
melees such as *The Bachelor* and *Meet the Folks*. But
more generally, for all its rhetoric of individual libera-
tion and icon-smashing, today's masscult landscape
greets outbreaks of actual audience subjectivity with
roughly the same ardor with which the Bush adminis-
tration greets solar energy proposals.

Today's typical masscult productions treat the
most frail and contingent features of individual life as
grist for formulaic contempt. Families are merciless
battlegrounds of generation and gender, dying is the
fate strictly reserved for losers, and emotional
responses of any kind are earmarked only for parody.
Much as it has translated urban experience into
generic suburban monoculture (à la *Friends* or *Sex and
the City*), masscult has set about extinguishing individual experience and replacing it with a stable of faux-
ironic gestures.

These themes converged in David Eggers'
ostensibly self-deconstructing best-selling memoir, *A
Heartbreaking Work of Staggering Genius*. In the book's

opening pages, the author efficiently tells the moving tale of his parents' deaths from cancer within three months of each other. Across the next tortured 400-plus pages, however, he systematically proceeds to distance himself from virtually all emotional accountability in the events he relates, and disarms the reader's trust in the narrator's moral compass. We learn that the garrulous self-narrating Eggers likes to come on to women in the wake of hospital visits to gravely injured friends; that he pretends to beat his younger brother for the sake of scandalizing a neighbor family; that he ditches a chronically suicidal friend on the San Francisco Bay Bridge just after retrieving him from the hospital in the wake of his latest attempt.

Most of all, of course, we are told (in so many words) that we are to look indulgently upon all these displays, because unlike the would-be earnest suckers known as his readers, Eggers has learned that his own suffering permits him to see through all illusions of mature comportment and deem all its attendant trials as fodder for more fastidious scorn. "Dignity is for pussies," he announces in a characteristic burst of Holden Caulfield-like bravado. It's meant to sound confrontational and daring, but in reality this sentiment could serve as the informal slogan of any number of similarly themed masscult offerings: the sneer-to-simper emotional range of sitcoms such as *Just Shoot Me* or *Malcolm in the Middle*; the creepy effloresence of death-themed ads for SUVs and nutrition bars; the bare-all cable-youth reveries of *Jackass* or *The Osbournes*; the endlessly allusive, casually nihilistic and character-resistant cinema of Quentin Tarantino and

Todd Solondz. The bulk of Eggers' memoir, in short, is TV on the printed page—compulsively wisecracking and self-narrating, suspicious of adult motives that might prove to be phony, and, above all, fearful of emotional engagement.

Eggers is also a representative hero of our time in another crucial respect: in repackaging trademark masscult reflexes, he also consolidated his position as a darling of the avant-garde—and indeed, as founder and editor of the self-congratulatory literary journal *McSweeney's*, one of its leading entrepreneurs. This is a dialectical synthesis unimaginable to the likes of Clement Greenberg. Rather than portending a dark age of fascist anti-intellectualism, today's open celebration of all things masscult has quietly absorbed whatever might remain of the avant-garde. In his own theatrically self-conscious way, Dave Eggers occupies roughly the same market position in his demographic that Oprah Winfrey does in hers: a synergistic brand that, by the simple logic of all personality cults, eclipses the homely distinctions of taste that might arouse suspicions about the Great Personality's claims to authenticity and cultural authority.

THE IMMEDIATE EXPERIENCE, REMEDIATED

This avant-enclosure might seem in line with various prophecies of the complete collapse of all taste and culture hierarchies in the omnientertainment age. John Seabrook's *Nobrow*, for example, argues that one-time high-culture sensibilities (typified for him by the fare traditionally published in *The New Yorker*) and the "low" culture media of tabloid gossip (whose essence Seabrook, not surprisingly, sees distilled in the pages of *Vanity Fair*) now exist in nearly indistinguishable states of mutual mimicry. A long, and still-multiplying, parade of academics have chimed in with much the same pronouncement, marveling continually that the once-oppressive gray and towering cathedrals of taste- and genre-distinction are now toppling everywhere at our feet. And through all this wonderment it still remains, of course, signal irony that the holders of high academic sinecures remain far more giddy about these developments than do mere journalists like Seabrook, who write for larger audiences.

But however it is greeted, this talk of runaway brow-flattening misses a key point, one that has long eluded many partisans in the masscult fracas: the division of culture hierarchies has always been different from the more fine-grained calibrations of taste. Taste moves independently through cultural hierarchy—which is now and has always been a very broad and imperfect sociological description of *audiences* rather than a set of fixed and undeviating magnetic poles that force this or that cultural offering into strict alignment with their cultural properties.

Thus a critic like Robert Warshow could simultaneously (and not unappreciatively) recognize the formulaic monotony of Hollywood movies—the means by which "originality is to be welcomed only in the degree that it intensifies the expected experience without fundamentally altering it"—while also castigating the no less rigid high-middlebrow canons of journalism in *The New Yorker*. Warshow noted, in his classic essay on the august weekly, that its editors had never expected, at the dawn of the atomic age, to face "a world in which inelegance could become so dangerous"; in response they developed "a special technique for handling what is directly threatening, and its function is the same as the function of [the magazine's] humor: to reduce everything to the point where the assumption of a simple attitude will make it tolerable."

Warshow's work, indeed, furnishes an indispensable occasion to see the great arid distance we've traversed since the time when individual taste was not obsessively privatized and quarantined, but instead associated with public virtues—and when cultural hierarchies were openly debated instead of reflexively reviled. From the vantage of today's reigning discourses on cultural matters, it is no longer possible to understand the logic by which Warshow ranged over such an obviously interconnected spectrum of high- and low- and middle-pitched cultural expressions.

Evidence of this is abundant, alas, in the presentation and reception of the 2001 reissue of his only book, *The Immediate Experience*. The book's jacket copy, instead of eliciting the language, method or topical scope of Warhsow's criticism, rushes to transpose it into the blinkered thumbs-up, thumbs-down sloganeering of our own age's thinly politicized cultural debate. Vaguely summoning the clash of Cold War ideologies for the sake of a certain dry-ice historical ambience, our jacket narrator then promptly assures us that "political correctness then, like political correctness since the 1960s, had led to 'organized mass disingenuousness' on the part of intellectuals who turned away from developing a vocabulary for describing the immediate, aesthetic experience and used irony instead, even about their own experiences."

Political correctness—check. Irony—check. Shifty self-regarding intellectuals—check. So

Warshow was like Robert Hughes meets Jed Purdy
meets Roger Kimball, only, like, in the Cold War, yes?

The only problem is that the poor reader
drawn in by this nonsensical, ahistorical sketch of
Warshow's career finds that the author does not berate
intellectuals for the betrayal of experience so much as
America's mass culture for failing to furnish the sort of
experience that not merely intellectuals, but poets,
novelists, and critics, can productively gestate and
transform into creative material of their own.
(Monotonous as it is getting to point this out,
Warshow, like most of the age's masscult critics, was
not some wilting and tweedy university "elitist," but
rather a lowly scribe who churned out essays for the
Partisan Review, *Commentary* and *The Nation*—and who
dropped dead of a heart attack just after accepting a
regular fulltime writing post at *The New Yorker*.)

Warshow did chastise the programmatic radicalism of many sloganeering '30s intellectuals, but
only because it reflected the wider flight from experience *already embodied in mass culture*. Sounding every
bit like Greenberg—whom he indeed quoted repeat-
edly and approvingly—Warshow wrote, "the chief
function of mass culture is to relieve one of the necessity of experiencing one's life directly." By contrast,
"serious art... is not an evasion: by its very detach-
ment, it opens up new possibilities of understanding
and pleasure derivable from reality, and it thus
becomes an enrichment of experience." And he goes
on to argue that "mass culture... seeks only to make
things easier. It can do this either by moving away
from reality and thus offering an 'escape' or by

moving so close to reality as to destroy the detach-
ment of art.... Even political discussion becomes a
form of entertainment: by providing a fixed system of
moral and political attitudes it protects us from the
shock of experience and conceals our helplessness."
Since so much of modern experience is formed out of
these de-subjectified mass materials, a crisis ensues for
"the modern intellectual, and especially the creative
writer [who]... faces the necessity of describing and
clarifying an experience which has itself deprived him
of the vocabulary he required to deal with it.... in a
sense, he must invent his own audience." A bit less
abstractly, Warshow insisted that this same rupture "is
the source of the problem of communication in
modern literature—which is a problem not only of
communicating the quality of experience to a reader,
but also, and more deeply, of making it possible for
the writer himself to have a meaningful experience in
the first place."

Political life grievously abetted this process, as
Warshow noted in an unforgettable essay on Julius
and Ethel Rosenberg. He argued that the notorious
spy couple had achieved an effective erasure of their
own identities, preferences, and the very intimate and
private qualities of their being, all in the service of a
debased Popular Front strategy of omnivorous appropriation of any and all liberal and patriotic cultural
tendencies:

> The point is that all beliefs, all ideas, all "heritages"
> were really the same to [the Rosenbergs], and they
> were equally incapable of truth and falsehood.
> What they stood for was not Communism as a cer-

tain form of social organization, not progress as a belief in the possibility of human improvement, but only their own identity *as* Communists or "progressive," and they were perfectly "sincere" in making use of whatever catchwords seemed at any moment to assert that identity—just as one who seeks to establish his identity as a person of culture might try to do so either by praising abstract painting or by damning it.

Warshow's "immediate experience" in other words, did not refer, as is now commonly asserted, to the uncomplicated and liberatory pleasures offered by mass culture; it referred rather to the struggle *against* the predigestion of cultural and political attitudes. Hence anyplace where he inveighs against the falsification of experience in political contexts, he almost always follows it up with a parallel illustration from cultural life. The deadened Popular Front sensibilities of the Rosenbergs and the knee-jerk diktats of culterati over abstract expressionism are but two sides of the same coin, which glibly recirculates the disturbing stuff of lived experience "to the point where the assumption of a simple attitude will make it tolerable." Like Greenberg and Macdonald, Warshow understood taste to be a vital bulwark against this process, shoring up the self's frail sense-making powers before the great flattening torrent of programmatic masscult.

This all bears revisiting at some length precisely because the analytic substance of Warshow's book completely eluded today's commentators on *The Immediate Experience*, of every political persuasion.

Leftist scholars, for example, deliberately lay

aside Warshow's own critical distinctions to make him the very sort of Popular Front sloganeer he derided the Rosenbergs for being. Henry Jenkins, Tara McPherson, and Jane Shattuc, the coeditors of a recent Duke University Press cultural studies reader, *Hop on Pop: The Politics and Pleasures of Popular Culture*, inappositely hail Warshow as a key progenitor of today's academic mass-cult ecstasies. Like most misguided appropriations of his work, this one proceeds from an opportunistic mis-reading of his book's title, making "the immediate experience" refer to something quite the opposite of the meaning Warshow intended the phrase to have. Instead of reporting that Warshow saw mass culture as the principal obstacle to immediate experience, Jenkins and company absurdly maintain that, "Robert Warshow developed a sociological theory of 'the immediate experience' of popular culture in everyday life.... He argued that there was no simple division between popular movies and art." Jenkins, McPherson, and Shattuc also go on to conscript Warshow into the front of another cultstud vanguard: the rise of the fan-critic. "Warshow advocated that the critics needed to take seriously the knowledge of the frequent filmgoer. In fact, he broke with the concept of intellectual distance which defined film criticism in the 1940s. The fan could be a critic and the good critic could only be steeped in film." To underline this claim, they quote from the mildly con-fessional introduction to *The Immediate Experience*: "I have gone to the movies constantly, and at times almost compulsively, for most of my life. I should be embar-rassed to attempt an estimate of how many movies I have seen and how many I have consumed." But typically they neglect to quote the next two sentences, which adumbrate the very distinctions that they claim Warshow tries to efface:

> At the same time, I have had enough serious interest in the products of the 'higher' arts to be very sharply aware of the impulse that leads me to the novels of Henry James or the poetry of T.S. Eliot. That there is a connection between the two impulses I do not doubt, but the connection is not adequately summed up in the statement that the Bogart movie and the Eliot poem are both forms of art.
>
> In other words: some fan.

Rather than blandly asserting the functional identity of high and low, or avant-garde and mass, Warshow hewed to the notion that his perception, subjective judgments and understanding—his taste—could be trained with equal vigor on any representative cultural production, regardless of its brow provenance. (Likewise, Dwight Macdonald, for all his alleged reflexive horror of mass culture, spent a great deal of time, and a lot of "serious" critical acumen, reviewing Hollywood movies.) Taste was a function of subjectivity; cultural hierarchy is a gauge of that subjectivity's erosion.

Not surprisingly, the force of this point is lost on the culture warriors on the right, just as it is on their leftish counterparts. Terry Teachout, reviewing the reissued Warshow book in *The Weekly Standard*, supplies a misreading identical to that of the *Hop on Pop* troika in every detail save its reverse-charged ideological brief. Where Jenkins, McPherson and Shattuc saw only self-made masscult elation in Warshow, Teachout

saw only ideology—and so further effaced Warshow's
insistence on the critical connection between masscult
debasement and Popular Front propagandizing.
Indeed, a propos of Warshow's Rosenberg essay,
Teachout writes that Warshow, unlike those Commie
posers, was the real-deal celebrant of masscult:

> Warshow's unfaked faithfulness to the immediate
> experience of the unpretentious genre films he loved
> stands in stark contrast to the falseness of Popular
> Front liberals who, like the Rosenbergs, approved
> only of art that served their political ends—an atti-
> tude that has since metamorphosed into what we
> now call political correctness. His essays show how
> the Stalinist habit of mind not only survived its evil
> inventor but has become part of the very essence of
> postmodern thought.

Well, no. For starters, Warshow's title referred
not to the substance of genre films, or any "unfaked
faithfulness" to same, but, as we have seen, to the very
kinds of direct experience that masscult genre films are
given to suppress, supersede and/or distort. And needless to say, this sort of inveighing over the horrors of
"political correctness" is the same crude attitudinizing
that made Warshow all but sputter with rage—and
indeed, bears a far greater resemblance to bootless
Popular Front posturing than does the "very essence of
postmodern thought" (which, being postmodern, can
scarcely be said to have much of an essence anyway).

Yet what's ultimately striking about Teachout's
conscription of Warshow into the ranks of latter-day
culture warriors is that it betrays exactly the sort of historical amnesia that Warshow and that other anti-
Stalinist masscult critic Dwight Macdonald warned

against. In particular, Teachout misunderstands the very quality in Warshow's work he deems so integral to it; Warshow's own anticommunism, or as Teachout far more ponderously puts it "the extent to which all his criticism was concerned with the long-term effects on American culture of the loose coalition of 1930s liberals, Stalinist fellow travelers, and full-fledged Communists known as the Popular Front."

In reality, one of Warshow's principal objections to the "habit of mind" that characterized Popular Front liberalism was its failure to reckon with the very kind of flight from historical detail that Teachout lustily undertakes in his own misguided appreciation. Warshow would in all likelihood cringe in sickly recognition over Teachout's deliberately obtuse identifications of Stalinism—which after all produced the planned murder and starvation of tens of millions of human beings—with such sweeping straw demons as "postmodern thought" and "political correctness."

In Arthur Miller's *The Crucible*, for instance, Warshow detected, despite all the play's pretensions to trans-historical "universality," a message that "belongs neither to literature nor to history, but to that journalism of limp erudition which assumes that events are to be understood by referring them to categories, and which is therefore never at a loss for a comment. Just as in *Death of a Salesman* Mr. Miller sought to present 'the American' by eliminating so far as possible the 'non-essential' facts which might have made his protagonist a particular American, so in *The Crucible* he reveals at every turn his almost contemptuous lack of interest in the particularities—which is to say, the reality—of the Salem trials."

One could imagine few better summations not merely of the historical mendacity of this Popular Front project, but also of Teachout's own patently false contention that left-wing anticommunism is "an affiliation which is (if possible) even less fashionable today than in the 1930s and early 1940s" and that "[t]oday, one is hard-pressed to find a leftist prepared so much as to acknowledge Stalin's existence, much less hint at the damning fact that his ardent admirers once played a hugely influential role in the shaping of American popular culture." One can't help but wonder if this guilt-by-dimly-asserted-association can be made to taint all leftist intellectuals, where might this leave our nation's president, who after all happily endorses new trade agreements with the world's largest Communist power and pals around on his ranch with the former head of the KGB?

This is all to say nothing about Warshow's own rather massively inconvenient socialist politics in the effort to rehabilitate his work as the dutiful output of a firebreathing anticommunist inquisitor. One reason he plumbed the delusions of the liberal mind so well is that, like George Orwell (whom Teachout also tries to transform into a Business Roundtable conservative of the 1950s) he knew them at close remove, from the unsentimental vantage of the left. And so Teachout, while dilating so tirelessly on Warshow's hatred of Communism, takes no note whatsoever of his marked contempt for right-wing shibboleths, as voiced, for example, in his eviscerating review of *The Best Years of Our Lives*. This Academy-Award-winning parable of post-World War II demobilization hinges, in Warshow's view, on a dishonest denial of "the reality of politics, if politics means the existence of real incompatibilities of interest and real *social* problems not susceptible of individual solution." Chief among these, not surprisingly, is the social problem of class:

> A conscious effort is made to show that social class differences do not matter. The infantry-sergeant is a banker in civilian life...; the Air Force sergeant is a soda-jerker, living with his workingman father in a miserable slum. The two men are presented as culturally equal: the soda-jerker can call the banker's wife by her first name and eventually marry the banker's daughter; this, too, is made possible by presenting everything as a surface, for the social equality of bankers and soda-jerkers is real—on the surface.

This work of surface-level class concealment enables an important piece of social mythology that Warshow also derides: namely, the pleasing American reverie that "the chief means of concealing the reality of politics is to present every problem as a problem of personal morality.... Thus the problem of the monopoly of capital is reduced to a question of the morals of banks: If bankers are good men, they will grant small loans (not large loans, apparently) to deserving veterans (those willing to work hard) without demanding collateral. (This is 'gambling on the future of America'; the small loan is apparently conceived to be some kind of solution to the economic difficulties of capitalism—cf. *It's a Wonderful Life*.)"

Perhaps Teachout isn't to be blamed for passing over Warshow's actual political commitments. In any event, it's scarcely surprising that he should do so, since such canny elisions are the stock in trade of the culture warfare of our day. But this does, at the very least, furnish another brief occasion to pause in wonderment before the funhouse mirror: We are being presented with a shrilly politicized portrayal of the thought of a critic who was devoted most of all to unmasking shrilly politicized representations of reality, in art and politics alike. Talk about your "almost contemptuous lack of interest in particularities."

And finally, of course, there's the great subject that Warshow attended to with such care, and that none of his contemporary readers appears even to notice: the taboo question of social class. Warshow's reflections on this subject—which appear not only in his dissection of *The Best Years of Our Lives* but in his essays on the gangster movie and the Western—are buried, and never to be exhumed, for the simple reason that the very idea of social class only enters into public notice today through the unlikely back door of culture.

SOUR TASTE

Much as our romance with mass culture has
swamped the frail remnants of what had been the
avant-garde, so has our politicization of taste made it
impossible to grasp in our public life what class continues to mean. Americans once understood that stub-
born social inequalities lie at the core of many of our
cultural disputes—which is why, indeed, we have
thought them to be properly addressed through the
palliative cultural power of education, long held to be
the chief engine of upward social mobility in America.
Now, however, we have stood that old consensus on its
head: We recognize and discuss class division only as it
putatively pertains to cultural division. We reflexively

endorse the curious notion that taste judgments and standards are the most significant correlates—if not, indeed, the leading causes—of much deeper divisions of the general population into social class. Even as one of the most wearisome American shibboleths holds that all taste judgments are subjective, we attend with insatiable interest to the alleged hardcore class affiliations those judgments are supposed to register.

Taste is indeed virtually the only realm in which the subject of class distinction gains any sort of hearing—albeit a hysterical and content-challenged one. The instant any hoarse liberal cry goes forth to protect Social Security from market predations, or introduce greater equity in the American tax structure, conservative propagandists howl in chorus on the indecent excesses of "class warfare." For most practical political purposes, there the matter ends. Yet turn away from these timid reformist debates and one beholds the entirely cost-free brand of *cultural* class warfare raging everywhere unappeased, with the mythical Unpretentious Folk vigilantly policing the speech and thoughts of the still more mythical Cultural Elites—as the instructive Oprah-Franzen dustup dramatized almost perfectly.

Indeed, the whole notion of exercising judgment (let alone—ye gods!—standards) is taken, in this debased class terminology, as evidence of unthinkably Old World and aristocratic snobbery, and so automatically calls down the holy retribution of an army of latter-day Edward Shilses, be it "bobo" funster David Brooks on the cultural right or the law-and-lit power ranger Stanley Fish on the cultural left. Access to cul-

ture is apparently universal—and indeed its ready
availability is taken to be the surrogate for the equal
distribution of more basic social goods—yet individual
efforts to make it meaningful, the critical assessments
and judgments that show the audience has its own
sweat equity in the definition of culture are, by the
game of culturalized class warfare, branded retrograde
forms of snobbery and oppression. In the conduct of
today's culture debates, taste distinctions are still
acknowledged, but only as the sign that the platitudes
of an allegedly globalizing mass culture are daily out-
growing the strictures of history. Judgments of taste
are usually invoked only for the sake of their formulaic
flouting of them as repressive, outmoded elitist tools
of domination; the notion that creators of culture can
speak to any general public beyond self-selected niche
markets and connoisseurs is laughably naïve in today's
culture market. Even as we're assured that our brave
new networks of masscult are feverishly globalizing
and ravenously eclectic in assimilating various "outsider" influences, our cultural life nevertheless remains
absurdly fragmented in its aesthetic ambition and sadly
insular in its social reach.

Serious discussion of taste judgments and aesthetic standards, very much by contrast, created the
vocabularies that were once common currency for a
now-vanishing cultural public. Standards are not top-
down impositions of effete and alien puppet masters
stage-managing the culture's progress, in the nature of
the off-screen alien race that delivers down the great
Monolith in *2001: A Space Odyssey*—such an image
could only gain widespread credence, indeed, when

deskilled culture consumers no longer recognize why taste matters. Far from trumpeting the virtues of pre-ordained consensus, taste standards are the outcome of—and the ongoing occasion for—public argument. The record of such arguments runs deep in the nation's history, from the early Republic's theological controversies to the 1920s literary insurgency against "the genteel tradition" to the civil-rights era's reconfigured mandates of civic responsibility. These expansive categories of debate cannot be made to square with the confrontational yet oddly depoliticized timbre of contemporary culture warfare: Once we have ceded the right to meaningfully air our own judgments and standards of taste in public, it turns out that we really have very little to talk about.

WHO DIED AND MADE OPRAH QUEEN?

This all became suddenly plain in the deflationary coda to our original Oprah-Franzen set piece: an unexpected, off-key, and Enron-like liquidation of cultural capital from our nation's greatest repository of literary marketing power. After vindicating her unilateral powers of culture arbitration in the Franzen battle, Oprah abruptly announced her own retirement from her Book Club. After six years of gratefully permitting this figurehead to speak as our good and great voice of literary consensus, we were rudely reminded that we hadn't really elected Oprah at all. She was a sovereign culture-monger, and she was choosing to exercise the fiat we had so long conflated with our judgment in the rather bald service of her own interest. "It has been harder and harder to find books on a monthly basis that I feel absolutely compelled to share," Dame Winfrey explained in an official statement. This terse account of unbidden book fatigue is itself a telling admission of a drastically narrowing cultural frame of reference. Oprah had, after all, made liberal use of backlist titles in her past selections—choosing no less than four entries by one living author, Toni Morrison, for instance. Surely, in conjunction with the more than 50,000 titles a year now being published in America, this stable of warhorses could yield a measly 12 titles a year to the discerning Book Club commissar.

Yet despite abundant evidence of Oprah's fickleness, many commentators still acted as though a crime of some sort had been perpetrated, and rushed again to pin the blame on Franzen. Writing in *The Nation*, Kathy Rooney—an academic at work on a thesis on the virtues of the Oprah Book Club—bemoaned the Oprah-Franzen affair as "a disheartening battle of egos between its figureheads... [that] led to an attendant galvanization along the lines of high and low culture in the population at large," of a piece with a wider "critical backlash against the selections of the club" that "presented unfortunate proof of how caught up in a kind of textbook hierarchy of legitimacy American literary culture really is." The club itself, Rooney argues, was nothing less than "a revolutionary cultural event," flattening the grimly authoritarian top-down business of traditionally levied critical judgments: "All reviewing of or advocacy for a particular book—whether it appears on the book's jacket, *The New York Times Book Review* or wherever else—may be construed as a suggestion or a subtle form of coercion from those in positions of cultural superiority to those at lower levels."

Note again the glib facility with which an opponent of taste hierarchies advances the strong connotation that American cultural publics are too delicate of constitution to greet any form of criticism (even the timid bouquets that publicists carefully arrange on book jackets) as anything other than sinister "coercion." But then all forms of criticism are, it seems, brute affronts to the Oprah Revolution: "Even though there are some who might say—and who did say—that the revolution should not have been televised, they were, quite simply and sadly, wrong, and now we're seeing the cost of their snide, misguided complaints.... Owing in no small part to this [i.e., Franzen's] highly publicized challenge to her cultural authority, Winfrey seems to have come now to the conclusion that the club is just no longer worth it, if it means being exposed to such derision."

One might expect that if such a decisive blow had been struck for cultural democracy under the Oprah brand, it wouldn't be the case that so much of the future of American literacy would be riding on a single talk show host's hurt feelings. One could protest, after all, that other cultural revolutionists, from Margaret Sanger to Leonid Trotsky to Marcel Duchamp, seemed to take public derision, and even "snide, misguided complaints," in stride—and without the consolations afforded by Oprah's estimated net worth of $425 million. Each of them—and of course, scores and scores of other, similar innovators—created actual cultural and political movements and schools. Oprah, meanwhile, has only bequeathed us the clamor of the *Today*, *Good Morning America* and *Regis and Kelly* book clubs.

Of course, if the Book Club had been the "revolution" of Rooney's fond imagining, it might well have survived the trauma of its charismatic Maximum Leader quitting the field. Rooney's claims of rampant taste bullying notwithstanding, throughout much of the history of American publishing, book clubs have been much sturdier and democratic in structure, with boards of writers and editors—obviously well-suited to absorb any number of high-profile comings and goings in their ranks—nominating a wide range of monthly offerings. A few clubs even mutated into full-time publishing operations themselves, as when the Psychoanalytic Book Club built enough of a subscriber base to be re-launched in the late 1950s as Basic Books.

Moreover, it's a bizarre misreading of the Franzen affair to cast Oprah as the defeated party. There were almost no public defenses of Franzen, and, as we have seen, no end of gleeful pillorying of the lone faithless egghead who Dared Criticize Oprah. If this was indeed an ill-starred clash of egos and figureheads, there's no doubt whatsoever who had the better of it, and whose "cultural authority" remained intact throughout. If Oprah walked abruptly away from her "revolution," it was precisely because she had acquired so much power and wealth that her sudden retirement would cost her nothing.

As usual, though, it was the publishing professionals—those ostensibly free-spirited, censorshipfighting impresarios of the marketplace of ideas—who purveyed Oprah-centric revisionism at its most thuggish. Here, for instance, is the author of "Publisher's Lunch," a weekly email alert on industry trends and gossip circulated under the aegis of Publisher's Weekly, with an impassioned *j'accuse*: "Like at least some of you, I really do blame Jonathan Franzen; but then anyone who has ever sniffed at one of her selections or whined about the Oprah sticker or any other such nonsense is also complicit."

For someone championing a populist icon of mass taste, this was an oddly inquisitorial flourish: The act of criticism was now cognate with ill-specified thought crimes. It makes perfect sense, though, given the tail-chasing agons over mass culture that we have been witnessing lo these past four-plus decades. Into the vacuum of a culture that no longer tries to challenge our imaginations, to replenish our understanding of the past, to engage the riddles of intimacy or redeem the dignity of our work, there can only reverberate the call-and-response din that promotes outsized celebrity adulation and denounces its putative betrayal. Even as culture disperses itself more widely and cheaply across the globe, even as technological innovations place the materials of learning more readily at hand to greater and greater numbers of people, there is a waning sense that culture is saying anything meaningful to us—or, for that matter, that we're demanding anything meaningful of it.

And small wonder, since the networks that own, produce, and transmit mass culture across the globe are bulking into an evermore cumbersome and top-heavy cartel, stamping out minor niche-marketed variations from an evermore inflexible, monocultural template. To be sure, the global cultural market now offers countless new points of access, but it has done so while standardizing its products in an unprecedented manner. Today's culture consumers find themselves haunting a cavernous pantheon of inert household deities—Oprahs, Rosies, Britneys, Backstreet Boys, O-Towns and J-Los, on up through the Eisners and Bruckheimers, Steve Cases and Bill Gateses who calibrate all the pertinent bottom lines and so have earned a celebrity all their own. All the while we are assured that we possess exponentially greater cultural choices than any known generation of Earth's inhabitants, and that suspicion to the contrary constitutes a faithless critical reflex that is either sadly delusional or borderline seditious. If culture itself arises from a set of distinctions—the sacred and the profane, the raw and the cooked, the pure and the dangerous, and even the "high" and the mass—how are we to characterize a new global culture that, in the very logic of its dissemination, makes it harder to assign any lasting value to its content?

But even to ask such a question is to betray a refusal to reckon with the great masscult absorption of all prior structures of feeling—the eclipse of the avant-garde, the empty politicization of aesthetic postures and the obsolescence of any and all publicly aired criteria of taste. Let the culture divide and recombine placidly over our heads; let culture warriors pout, rage, preen and triangulate; let us glory indiscriminately in a market we never made; let a thousand Oprahs bloom. It's lullaby hour in red and blue America. ■

Look for these titles by Prickly Paradigm, and others to come: